CW00860221

ZJ GALOS

# DIARY OF AN AGED APRIL

a month in the life of a poet

on the southern hemisphere

poetry & drawing

impressum

Bibliographical information of the German National Library.

The German National Library indexes this publication with the German National Bibliography. Detailed bibliographical data may be derived from the Internet website http://dnb.dnb.de

© 2021 Z J GALOS

Printed and publisher: BoD - Books on Demand, Norderstedt.

ISBN: 9783754323861

aged april

Description of content

The poet has lived and worked in the South of Africa for a long period of time.

During his tenure in the design and supervision of buildings: domiciles to offices, industrial buildings, technical workshops for the maintenance of airplanes, clinics and laboratories, workshops for heavy turbine equipment and hospitals, he had a whole life devoted to it, until one day he was out of architectural work.

He had always been drawing from fantasy as a counter effort to foster his love for creative artwork.

Photographic explorations went hand in hand with exploring the African landscapes. The moment his work had been completed, he met with friends who shared the love for poetry with him. Besides meeting them in an Art-Café in San Francisco, he met poets in Athens, Greece, and many talented poets from Europe and all over the world on the Internet, where he conducted a website, called WordPress.com for his blogging and journal poetry.

During his last year in Africa he met his love interest, he exchanged poetry with. While he has honoured her wish to keep his poetry – resulting from their 'love at distance' – private, he felt for the need for its intensity of exchanges to become public only, when his Muse had passed away.

'Once the ink had dried, - to state the poet's phrase – he would edit and prepare this intense physical and spiritual high-flying month during April 2010, where he worked on his manuscript from April 2004, to offer this unusual inner life-poetry to the public.

The quotation 'Tempus fugit' is indeed the speediest experience in matters of love. "You cannot put your foot twice into the same water" paraphrased from Herodotus, states this toward all happenings of history that since had changed the lives of many people in the region of Southern Africa.

Index of Content:

"intercession"

   do racial tensions rise by
flying the old four colour-flag?
   do hate speeches feed on
the poison of political greed
the anger of people not being
served due to the incapability
of local government to deliver
as promised?
  where are the leaders who
are true to the democratic idea
as championed by emerging
hope/ raised by the nation's
new 'rainbow-children'
who support the symbolized
idea?
   the positions have hardened
and racialism is neither in flying
a nationalistic flag
nor in a song of denouncement
hate/ or a threat of killings.
   what is the real issue then?
it's the flag we all fly in our hearts.
could we all become compatriots?
   the rainbow has faded
songs and slogans sizzled sparks
igniting a war visually/ which roams

across the land.
where are the renewed connections?
   are some speeches protected and
others aren't?
   what flag will then be raised in midst
the overall population?


                    *

april 1

*symbols & models/*

*hanna*

the skeleton of youth fell

from the white cupboard

it smelled of mould and rotten wood –

life as a manuscript rolled open

heaped-up with detailed researches

on buildings and art –

kupka/the artist's face/gaunt/

all bones and skin

but his paintings move in circles

and abstract symbols like

mystical worlds made visible.

marie who thinks to be my model

for a nude in a czech adventure

opens up to me all of a sudden

having known the enigmatic artist

while valery the russian writer

transforms my language into a novel

with his russian mother-tongue –

don't worry/he soothes my

overheated mind/it'll be finished –

but of course

not before elena/sandstone girl/

has read it

she lives stretched-out and chiselling

through veins of gold and quartz

pure like a mountain spring

whispering like a gentle breeze

her doe eyes always shine

like gems.

he's all bones and skin,

but his gems are poetry & art.

*

## april 2

*natasha*

   the woman with a mystic
smile/ who promises my horoscope
for free
as if there would be anything for
free/ other than love for love-
pursues stars and predictions
to hook me up for her wizardry.
   natasha appears from the company
which moves one's possessions
across the oceans in steel containers
locked up but not safe from somali's
pirates,/ waylayers of the twenty-first
century.
   b. would cry if her Victorian pieces
would be sailing into nowhere...
natasha measures up with efficiency
giggles at my comments/ laughs
adjusts her loose/ white cotton top
continually – perhaps i stare at her
hidden boobs below
assess her body like an artist
perhaps I feel attracted to her in this
intimacy of opening all cupboards

my personal possessions to her:
my life in detail/ past girlfriends
loves and muses' paraphernalia.
  she takes a bookmark of my last
published book I hand her as my
innermost/ her eyes turn warm
and glisten...
we kiss like friends on cheeks.


*

april 2 ctd

*hanna*

   the dream is life/ as africa
is supported on a cane
an aged man walking stooped.
   life is a dream as painters
scatter white paint all over
boundary walls
which reflect the light like
an army with polished shields
turning them against a deluxe
car and a man from the agency
who appears aggressive
making money in another home
he'll prostitute.
   i lie in bed supine and hanna
will descend from rain swept
heavens for another night in
pleasure. i close my eyes, she
let's me sleep/ gather strength
for a sexual recharge:
cellphone life.
   she loves me/ therefore I am
still. b. loves me as my best of
friends and partner for a life-long

game staying afloat on the raft
that'll sweep us along to much
gentler shores
far away from the dark lands
where dusky circe holds me
in her ban
at times like a black magic
woman.

'where are you going?' the tall
worrier of society asks.

'to greece,' i reply and he looks
forelorn/ a deep fold builds on his
forehead reaching to his nose.

'maybe to austria'/ i put him off.

'salzburg i like'/ rona the sweet
hearted woman assistant says.

'i do not know where i'll go/ it's
a circle i am travelling in. it might
come to a close in athens
below the sheer face of the
'sacred rock'/ on the glass floors
of NAM- in the embraces of the
muses/ in the archaic smile of the
kore/ in a hug of marble to come
alife: aphrodite encumbered/ but
most beautiful in her appearance
that radiates from hanna's love.

'what do you want for your property?'

"i want two million.' this stops the
agent with his swelling fold

in his tracks.

  'you asked me,' I say and do not listen
to his counter arguments. he'll play
me down/ i know.

  'well let the market then decide.'
b. is disappointed/ it's a great shock
for her.

  'we'll need a top price for our
last raft, we'll float upon.
everybody would.

  'i'll market it that way/' the agent
says/ while we'll wait for our last
months in africa.

*

NAM – New Archeological Museum (Athens).

symbols & models/ hanna

april 2
*in afterthought/ resurrection.*

   it is easter. i do not feel '
the joy of it. i recall resurrection
a symphony by mahler
the pergolesi/ anna sent me
the importance of being reborn
in mind and body through
pains of love/ as i sort letters
paging through passages in my
life. amazement/ inner tremors
joy of having travelled to
historic places
sensational rides since many
years.
   aches in memories of past loves
i denuded myself for, renewed like
a child of apollo for hanna
virtual loving luxuriant vibha
big busted d'elle
embracing friends for life.
   night for night hanna will be
straddling me.
day for day africa's skies fade
into this ageing easter.

the sun has left afrique du sud.
africa is dying.

april 3
carl

  carl has risen from his
hibernation on a grey day
with grey clothes,
grey skies that douse our
faces with mist and it wets
my hair I keep tied in a
ponytail
while he folds his woollen cap
around his shaven head.
  to empty my studio feels
like cutting through my life
with a serrated knife:
all the tons of paper
reams of poetry
heaped up on the floor
i have to pack into black
refuse bags
with files of my past existence
as a project manager
designer of domiciles and odd
offices/ draftsman of proper
working drawings
architect for the middle class.
  carl hangs–on to the damaged
chandelier/ a cane dog's basket

and whatever he wishes to
enjoy what we've enjoyed once
when we had dogs.
    despite the cold we drink
windhoek drafts and munch
pizza with a chilli dressing
discussing life in general that has
turned against the minority
population and crime that is
tolerated by the authorities.
    in terms of our professions
we talk the same language
in real life I have the edge over
him with my projections
i've worked and moulded
into a future unseen to him


                    *

april 5
seven muses

   the dance of stars aligns
to the day's significance in numbers
in reduction to be anna's seven.
   selene will join the nocturnal
celebration/ as Apollo plays the lyre.
   from various spots around the world
muses of poetry/ music and dance
will join the poet's quest for a
loving union.
   i will sing their names for the ritual
of spring in the clouds:
            anna/ the greek muse
            hanna/ aphrodite's child
            halina/ angel of light
            elena/ the glow of wisdom
            eesha/ the passionate hetaerae
            agi/ the temperamental gypsy woman
            dingsen/ porcelain doll from shanghai.
we dance in a circle we all wish to
close to one ring of iron
made of human warmth
flesh and bone
mixing our all white blood.

                    *

natasha

april 6
*packing-up home*

   and in the morning
i empty my pad/ studio
and private space
that's becoming public now
   with an impersonal touch
hiding my writing away/ my
collections of pens/ laptop
cd's and works of art
turning into a contemp
bedouin/ like carl/ who has
a temp home/ renting space
from a friend with his two
cats and cctv
he collects ancient household
items/ light shades and old
lamps.
   i bring him my plum cake
he barbeques the meat.
his first wife brings him plates
and salads/ balsamico and
olive oil.
   carl reads aloud from a
biography on hemingway
while lisa buys a copy of my
book/ novel one. i'm glad.

yet i feel estranged from a
country that could not become
a home to me and neither to
b. how hard will it be to sell
our well-maintained home?

*

## april 7
*violent land*

   my waking of non-excitement
into the rain of her tears
that wash the red clay off
caked blood from the disc of
eros/ who has hurt his wings
in a hijacking attempt.
   my disappointed morning
passed the long stretched
empty spaces of broken land
abstaining from the glow of
the once lush african lands.
   my sudden austerity in a lost
diet of softened oats and
dried fruit that swills
like a wave in a flood
buckets pouring from desolate
heavens having lost its blue.
   my feelings in a turmoil
of having faded like the paint
of the sky's billboard
advertising paradise at the
indian ocean.
   my body left behind like an
empty shell for one crab to
take possession like a hermit

lick all up like a scavenger-
no - it's your tongue
your fingers that dig me back
into life.

*

april 9
*cracking-up*

I'm cracking up at my
lower back
like the plaster on my
studio wall
which could not take
the temperature changes
of a cold and humid april.

I'm crackin' up like two
different parts
not fitting any longer –
the top is cool writing
poetry
while the bottom's hot
seeking sexual merging.

the pages i am opening
are matching elite women
all successful in monetary
terms,
but then only on the free
porn page.
i can see a French woman
making love
just as i'd like it too.

i write a *lettre bleu* to hanna
reflecting sexual love
at its best
feeling relaxed having entered
a repose
stopping me to crack up
completely.

*

seven muses

april 10
*michaela*

  work physically to a sweat
ride a bike all the way to
see the place where i was born.
  in the early morning i feel
the pain of labouring along
familiar roads
i used to travel once by the
red bus to the capital
studying architecture and
fine art.
  more so to escape the vice
of labour for one man
toughened up by war,
toughening me up
working the fields he
inherited from his parents
haystacks of emotion he
collated to burying his feelings
inside
while i rushed to the early
afternoon bus
to keep my rendezvous
with michaela
whose huge brown eyes
eyed me/ being a denuded nymph

in the vienna woods
painted in stark autumn colours.
   her clothes like falling leaves
sliding sweetness through
awakening hearts.
   a push of mean waylayers
brought me to a fall
my bike hurled into the
undergrowth.
   i wake to the warble of the
bull-bull
the busy-body bird: cheeky
indian mynah
bouncing me back into life.

*

## april 11
### poet of love

   time has crusted over wounds
of the heart
has time healed unfinished love?
   years of sadness have shed
their tears on the dusky lands
and flooded low-lying fields.
have years of sadness passed?
   love emerges from the mist
of the high ground above
'white waters'
calling with a seductive song
an excited bull-bull
tossing his tail feathers about.
   lust is love, you have once
written to me in a chain of letters
i've carefully collated and kept
accessible at all times
   wishing then to be known as
poet of love
dwelling in your sweetness
feeling such great desires
as if a teen again
starting out to discover
love's joys and its pains.
   love/ sweet love in its

endless variations
having it lost
buried below ground
finding it again with fervour
in its ever presence
of great longing
in this sacred pilgrimage.

*

## april 12
### selling one's african home

   slaving for a presentation
selling one's home is a milestone
nightmare
waiting for a buyer
being hammered down in one's
expectation.
   what are we doing here in
such a strange land
where shadows crowd the hills
the skies
blocking out the rays of the sun?
   crouching on my knees
burning like stung by a bee
painting the studio walls/ awful
it is to me/ interrupting creative
quality time.
   why can't the spirit dwell in a
weathered marathon's' beach house,
undisturbed
rushing my pen over paper?
   i hate to be a slave for people
who are still stone age men –
entirely ignorant of basic education –
though there's no lack of libraries.
all it needs is a will

*not bashing-in heads*
*or killing for the sake of*
*acquiring mobile phones.*

*

selling one's african home

## april13
### creativity

   the poet in deep thought
cleans out the drawers of
his mind.
pictures of the past
celebrated life: in love
he is endowed with riches
eros has bestowed on him.
   dark spots of destruction
seeped into the walls
that are protective of him
for half of his adult life.
   he'll paste them up and
paint the white of impersonality
over his creative walls
he's decorated with such
spirited rushes/ bursts of
creativity he'll stash away
into the words
he's burning in a hurry onto
discs for conservation:
   love letters/ erotic drawings
words of spontaneous lewdness
gentle lyrical songs/ longing
desire and passion.
   restless with his fingers shaping,
modelling/ creating.
the poet is still.

april15

he lives in the country's green
consulting a man from the AA
who uses google earth to depict
his farmland in bright colours
on his monitor.
'what are you looking for jens?'
i ask/ the small child asleep
in his broad arms.
he looks forlorn as he gazes
at his land which might be one day
attached by the state and taken
from him
maybe not while madiba is still alive.
'where are you going?'
wide-eyed jean/ who maintains
my roof/ peeling off the weathered
membranes/ asks.
'i'm moving to greece'/ I say
as he looks at me like the child
in jens' big arms/ but with the
face of an old man.
'oh you have no plans?'
his doe-eyes back, he shakes
his head.
'while you are still young
you can take this here/ I reply.

he nods/ but I am too old for
staying longer on this barren
rock of gold/ i add.
he smiles like a young boy
his life cut out for him with
an uncertain future -
just like mine.

*

## april 15 night
*where love art you?*

  i feel like a stranger
reading my first manuscript
of 'fervour'/ amber of my
innerness.
slowly i feel my way into
bygone times.
  oscar plays a boogie-blues
funky, with the same passion
as i write.
from him to himera/ passed
jarrett and back again to the
master
funky and burning in his
chords of fire
all consuming like love.
  hanna will cook all-delicious
soups
her generosity for love is real
and healing for me
  while agi takes my hand
taking on the role as virtual friend
who is in love
but then is she?
  lia was genuinely interested in
offering her bed, while the poet

had been weeping for his dead
muse/ becoming an involuntary
witness to a necklacing in africa
tragedies emphasized by news
about earthquakes.
   where love ar't you?
   where will the poet come to
an inner peace?

                    *

creativity

## april 16
### africa addio

a helicopter circles above my head,
its rotor blades whip-crack the air.
all birds scatter from the garden's
tranquil recluse.
   i have travelled the boundary walls
of my african existence
for many years,
for endless years behind exile's
self-imposed fences
which now come finally to an end.
   falling from the skies above me
helicopter fumes as acid rain,
a galloping white horse races
from its night star's shine
snatching at me with its giant
teeth
pulling me up to a night ride
which leaves me breathless and
exhausted – i am falling – sliding-off
its slippery back
   crashing through the hot tin roof
at high noon
my back in pieces/ until dawn
i call for help to hermes-toth
spiritual healers of a poet

placing me together again
for your warm hands that'll
ease me into pleasure and back
and fro we rock into a new day:
another gift of love
in the knowing smile
of eros.

*

## april 16 evening
*ménage-a-trois*

   and how are the girls today
in their ménage-a-trois?
heh? She's puzzled-it's a
metaphor – heh –
indeed i can sense her pain
not ready for either tease
or dispute.
   i received an oil painting
today/ she said
   what style?
   it's in red and partly abstract
i do not like red/ she muses
i like blue.
   i call you blue then/ blue in
your existence/ I say.
   i do not feel well/ she says,
i dislike people and their talk:
do not smoke!
i smoke, but i do not like it
she says
   i guess i understand svety
with her tested nerves
her slow disintegration that will
run not later than to this autumn
indeed/ she's not well.

    i am sick of life/ she says
i want to sleep and not wake up
anymore.
    i hug and kiss her like a muse
i need to paint with my two
other muses/ as a friend of
sweethearts
so well becoming for the poet.

                    *

## april 17
*the red/black chinese notebook*

   I eat like a poet:
self-cooked food/ carefully marinated
grilled slowly.
   i look like a writer:
unshaven, but clean/ pedantically clean.
   i draw you as close as i am able to:
sliding my flat hand into your
unbuttoned dress/ onto your warm skin
and below to tufts of hair with
slippery moisture
below the hill of venus
into a groove suiting my fingers
stroking you with sexual greed
as you open up for me more and
more
   i fall to my knees to eat you
tasting your innermost soul
where a red pinhead of desire
greets me for my tongue to taste
and to love
in my show of tenderness
until red lust will take over
   in explorations of our love
we express our desires/ all of them
one by one

i will touch your quim/ all-over
moist by now/ your knobbly nipples
push forward
their broken discs like armour
   we could carry-on forever-
i need to feel them on my palms
brush over them and kiss them
greedy to swallow the greater part
of them
take-in as much as I can
   uh! i need this/ you say
   i do too! i echo.
   how sexy when you touch yourself
you say/ my pussy is still moist from
before/ let go/ for it's up to you now
oh/ well done for a quickie! hug/ hug...
   we needed this before we depart
for a week's break
but i will buzz your phone at times –
just so you know that i thought of you
see you in bed love!
   yes/ yes/ see you soon.


                         *

yesterday's song of intimacy
had me all enticed
as soon as i went to bed with you
late at night
i felt sweet tension of pain and
lust.

*

i draw your life and mine into the
red poetry book
as we have met in cosmic space
before
body parts crystallizing from
orbiting matter
formed from the souls of our
loved ones' before us.

*

*ménage-à-trois*

## april 18
at the med's shores

   mornings are gentle at
times/ like this one i wake into
your spirit has touched me with
love
   in unison with birdsong
and the music of rodrigo
sounds of four guitars on a
sunday morning/ when I need
to drift with you together
   above the clouds of a
med's blue/ where pieces
of land are scattered
into innumerable islands
like body parts
that desire to be unified.
   sailing at times close
and feel the underlying drift
of passion play
pushing us onto the shores
   beaching up like sacrificed
fish/ chosen by the
*dodeka theotites*/ gods for
another phase of creation
one that pains within the
effort of unifying our missing

other halves
one that holds deep promises
for great lust
the cherry on top.

*

dodeka theitites – twelve deities.
(greek mythology)

april 18.later
*merging*

...i'm washed away by rain
you take my wetness in
my soaked love
that has not faltered
thawing up
rising in you like dough
   your fingers kneading me
i feel alive again
wetting your sensual appetite
embracing the marble of your
skin
bouncing back the desire for
love that creates two more
faces
in this beautiful triad of your
emotions that overpower me
digging into me from your
supreme magical powers
i am dematerialized from
   floating like flotsam on the
med's stirred up blanket
that you have doffed at your
rebirth from its lapping folds
and foam-created
you surround me
in this most unusual merging.

## april 20
café with two red zeros

  swishing sounds of espresso
steamed from the sleek machine
in between cluttering of cups
that are heaped up yet to be filled
and served again and again.
  the foam-born idea like a venus
aphrodite in endless disguises
lives among the artist/ the poet
the piano player/ the scribe of
history
seen through his eyes
never as brutal/ or barbaric
as the wiping-out of many millions...
   some names remind of terror
others of gruesome deeds
into the vacuum of a non-existent
café-society/ the poet suffers
withdrawn like from the warmth
of a woman's womb
her body's closeness
the daily sensation of
sensuous skin
shared the way
magnets click together.
  in a café with to red zeros
ticked-over by dupoi's old clock

its roman numerals in a bold
circle have long survived
but for the better?

*

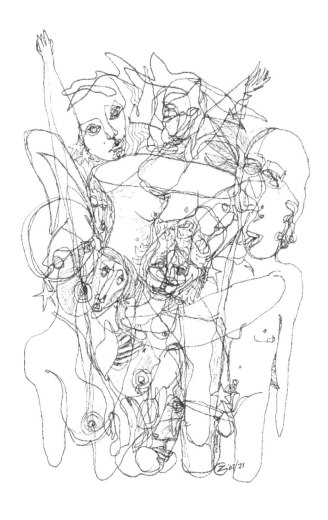

merging

## april 21
*one arm artist*

  frozen shoulder –
pulsing video of a grand
concert piano brought to
life with one arm,
five fingers that race over
keys and dance with many
that jump from the strung
wires with great talent
playing *caravan*
set the desert sand across
the eyes of all jazz cats that
are transported with an
unseen chain on the back
of a ship of music that
dematerializes fingers/ arms
clothes and bodies
to float on its pulsing love
up into the clean air of a
warm land
its waves of the sea in amber
sand that rises and turns
into incredible shapes
through a fata morgana
becoming the colourful caravan
with mirrors on dresses
and turbans on dusky heads

a celebration between corns
of sand that assembled into
rocks
and a sweet-water oasis
emerging –
frozen shoulder.

*

## april 22
eleusis

   my frozen constellation:
your loving caress for my
erection.
   one armed/
my upper body a mutilated
torso of sleek marble
dug out the sacred precinct
   of Eleusis
half-dead/ half-alive
merging pointed touches
in a waking-up process
within a smaller circle of
human relations
in a dance of well-rounded
muses
   their emotions conducted
by the poet's passion
with longing and desire
overlapping all minds.
the music of geometry
reflects great excitement.
the floating carnival
the mirage
through the looking glass
of my restless soul.

## april 23
is love death?

   brothers are splitting hairs
and even if they are gods
one of them splits the other one's
head with an axe
creating goddess *athena* in full
armour
protecting her chosen city,
   leaving us mortals the headaches
the migraines/ the splitting pains
of existence
at times as it is with b./ who is in
continual fights to stay alive/
without the help from mortals
knowledgeable in medical science
and skilled in surgical procedures
   without laughter/ tears flowing
in a depressed state
leading to departures of mind and
body
seeking death and yet with some
hope for relief
for life is given only once.
   taking some acid/ some downers/
some pain relief muti/ even if it
kills on the other side of life.
   The poet muses about death

while he still pursues his longing
for love.
  is love death?


                    *


muti – a general south african tribal expression for a
       medicine-man's healing potion.

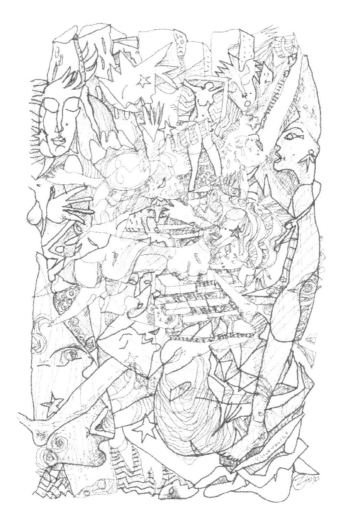

is love death?

## april 24
*life & death*

   since one week now/ ash clouds
formed a blanket across europe
there are no flights
   while here on the southern tip
of africa/ rain is pelting down for
days on end.
   all night the downpipe sings
its drumming song
of the pains of growing old
   the colours of africa have faded
into the meltdown's mist from
'eternal ice'.
   everything 's changing without
special announcement/ without
respect to man
   but man had little or no respect
to his natural habitat/ he destroyed
in an irreversible process.
   in gory pictures of life and death
hope and deception
the war of religions leaps ahead.
   i am searching for loyalty
love between cyber-highways
that has flowered like a seed
grown in a crack between split
concrete slabs.

the land below our feet
shakes in tremor –
man has dug for gold
far too deep.

*

## april 25
cyber-loving

   longing for love
craving for her flesh
biting off from her body
feeling horny like a cannibal?

   longing for a tête-à-tête
dancing on her stretched-out
body like her desired man
lover man
not throwing any tantrum

   in love's tension with the
comm.s window not opening
entirely up at times
seductive words will be
absorbed
by white nothingness

   masturbation's monitor
in a full screen mode
will lead to as many happy
couples in love
as varied speeds of fucking
as changes of positions

   but all of that might be

quite stimulating
your remembrance from
similar acts
through words written down
in a moment's heat of
fornication
having more power over
soulmates than raw porn

   your presence in the latest
novel swells my cock and its
awakening fire flashes through
my chest –
how sweet Tao exercises could
bring me to a close height
carrying on with hanna –
as in anna with an h in front
and you'd be smiling with
this threesome
I know you'll do.

*

april 26
want/grab/taste

you stir me with your
sensual pleasure while
i press my thighs together
as if i would feel you now
it's the same feeling i had
when we met for the
first time –
we both wanted it
wanted to grab it
taste it
consume it –
it has not left me
even if at times it is
crusted over by daily haste
the worries about an
uncertain future
it is back again
with a heartbeat.

\*

cyber loving

## april 27
grand slide

   tweet, tweet, the bird like sound from
the stand-by power pack
gives up life
the energy source dies
   a cold wind is needling my skin
drawing blood like a swarm of bats
   i flee back into my carapace's shell
still pleasant from the body warmth
of a night with my muse
my extended erotic self
   no need for an avatar with her
no need for protocol or
artificial sex enhancers
   the warm touches from her hand
her breasts will chafe my body
into a stretch
she shapes into this dildo
she'll inset into her body's openings
one easier sliding into than the
other's narrow passage
   never tiring i will be woken into
the armour of love's bitter-sweet
battles
   the sweat and tears of conquering
my love in her cries
falling from the morning star's

glitter
in a grand slide upon slippery
paths
we'll dance skin to skin's
afterglow passion.

*

april 28
passion as final act


   there is a sound in the air
this morning
as if someone beats an object
that is hollow
   as if there is a connection of
places seen that relate to each other
in magical precision
thought out many thousands of
years ago.
   when you could be a receiver
of these pictures of the world's
sacred precincts.
   your muse will transform from
her mind into yours
even if the world would topple
upside down.
   the omphalos of human emotions
will draw your ear to the seductive
sounds of your muse.
   your calling is confusing to you
and yet love is the motor for your
existence
the clock to be rewound
passion to be rekindled
   as a final act before
you'll die?

## april 30
*aphrodite encumbered*

night with a 1000 eyes
above a bay of molten
silver sea
beach-dogs like shadows
behind the fist of an
old boat in defiant pose
against a spook of
ancient wall
still crumbling into
pieces of stone
which move like heads
as a door opens
creaking in its worn hinges
and cat-eyes glow like fire
swept-up from a night's
high tide
leaching  crumbs of plaster
from the ancient wall for
a peek into the fisherman's
life inside/ who was
once a princely man from
the west
falling victim to the
purple gang who
squeezed him into chains
of a lifelong dependency –

a revenge of the jealous god
with the three-thronged spear –
be it as it may but piercing in
love will never fade –
king or god   rich man   poor man
beggarman   thief or be it
honey-kissing lina   muse of
critical review of prose and
restless agi    puszta fire in
her belly
cynical svety travelling to
greece pursuing her other
half in love
h.m. soulmate and lover
extraordinaire
aphrodite encumbered...
the warmest human being
embodiment of passion
inspiring sweet lewdness
in the poet who observes
the greek muse crying.

*

aphrodite encumbered

About the author

Born in Eastern Austria, close to the Hungarian border, he witnessed as a young man the horrors of a nation's suppression, erupting in the Hungarian Revolution of 1956. He finished his education in art and architecture in Vienna, married, and sailed for the Cape of Africa, an adventure that followed his childhood dreams. He had drawn African animals for his art classes, but the time had come to see them in their natural habitat.

Meeting a varied facet of people and cultures, working as a draughtsman in an engineering office, as an architect for a cultural centre, as a coordinator of craftsmen and professionals, he made good use of his language skills traveling throughout Southern Africa.

During a trip to Lesotho, a native artist showed him rock paintings with their stark palimpsest outlines and with typified movements of animals and humans. It made a lasting impression on him and influenced his artistic work.

His vast collection of drawings and slides had been lost during a change of domiciles, but further studies of the art of the San-people reawakened his dormant artistic longing for expression of his art, filling sketchbooks with drawings and notepads with poetry and prose. While revisiting the capitals of Europe, he sensed the bond of art being borderless and free, reaching out across continents into the world.

During a visit to Greece, he was accepted into a circle of artists and poets, who encouraged him to continue his art and a friend introduced him to the works of famous Greek poets.

In South Africa, he joined writing and poetry workshops of *Writers Write*. It was to open the floodgates of his creativity.

He decided to travel through Greece and visit its sites of antiquity, read up on Classical mythology, and enjoy translations of Greek poetry and prose.

He settled in 2013/14 in Klosterneuburg-Weidling. Poet Nikolaus Lenau is buried here. Franz Kafka had visited here. Their writings will always be an inspiration.

Books by the author in English:

King of Ice – A poetic legend
The Fabricator – Life and death for a great canvas
Spleen of Love – Zen and the Lake Moeris Adventure
Acropolis – Book I: Fervour
Fighting Stance – Triangulation in Love
Zora's Mistake – The potential of a hidden error
Athens Elegies – A poet's lament
The Mill below Owl castle – Zol's Sentimental education.
Educating Pizzy – The Artist Evolves
Short Stories Part I – From a writer's workshop. Book I/II
The Vivenot Elegies – Along a murmuring brook
Short Stories Part II – Book III/IV
Two Loves – Adventure in Eros
Short Stories Part III – Perpetual Eros. Book V/VI

Books in German:

Der Fabrizierer – Leben und Tod für ein großartiges Gemälde
Zoras Fehler – Das Potential eines versteckten Irrtums
König vom Eis – Eine Poetische Legende.

Lightning Source UK Ltd.
Milton Keynes UK
UKHW020631300821
389708UK00009B/463